ROOTS AND BRANCHES

First published in the UK in 2007 by
Two Rivers Press
35–39 London Street
Reading RG1 4PS
www.tworiverspress.com

Two Rivers Press is a member of Inpress.

Design: Nadja Guggi

Printed and bound by Richfield Graphics, Reading

ISBN 978-1-901677-54-6

Two Rivers Press gratefully acknowledges
financial assistance from Reading Borough Council.

ROOTS AND BRANCHES

THE CENTENARY HISTORY OF BATTLE AND CAVERSHAM LIBRARIES, READING

BY DAVID CLIFFE

TWO RIVERS PRESS

THE PUBLIC LIBRARY MOVEMENT

There is no logical reason to celebrate centenaries. It happens only because human beings have five digits on each hand, so we count in tens. Yet we have always felt the occasional need for jubilees and anniversaries – to stand back, and celebrate our achievements, and think about where we are going. Ten times ten is a good round figure. The shelves of the Local Studies Collection at Reading Central Library have many centenary histories – of societies, of churches, of companies, of train and bus services – so why not one for these two libraries, which were built within a few months of one another in 1907–08? They have many things in common, and many differences. It was a pity that in 1983 the opportunity was not taken to celebrate the foundation of the first rate-supported public library in Reading with a history. At the time, the librarians were preparing to move into the new Central Library, of course. This book will hopefully go some way to making good the omission.

The first Public Libraries Act was passed in 1850. It allowed boroughs with a population of over 10,000 to provide library buildings, though not books – it was assumed that these would be donated. The product of a ½d. rate could be levied, and the councils had to consult their ratepayers before deciding to adopt the Act.

This Act followed the deliberations of a House of Commons Select Committee the previous year. The Committee considered the limitations of the access people had to books and journals, and compared it, unfavourably, to provision in continental Europe and the United States. There was provision if you could pay, of course – most towns had subscription libraries, circulating libraries, and mechanics' institute libraries.

By the time Reading began to consider building a public library, in the 1870s, there was the Athenaeum Library in Friar Street – the building was demolished when Queen Victoria Street was cut through about 1900 – and the Southern Counties Library, run by George Lovejoy from 37–39 London Street, now the Reading International Solidarity Centre. By this time, the Literary, Scientific and Mechanics' Institute, which kept a library at the hall in London Street (now the Great

Rainwater head, Battle Library

Expectations hotel, restaurant and bar), was defunct, and the hall had become a Primitive Methodist chapel.

Twenty years before that, when the first Public Libraries Bill was under consideration, Parliament was extremely busy – the country was in a state of turmoil, with population increasing, industrial towns expanding, railways being built, and the great need becoming apparent for improvements in infrastructure, public health, social welfare, education, and so forth. Levels of literacy were low, and it was estimated when an Education Bill was being drawn up in 1850, that less than 8% of the nation's children attended school. Public libraries were to be especially for those who had missed out on education – 'the schoolrooms of grown-up men.' They would give the 'grown-up men' an alternative to the public house, and they would need to open late into the evenings. At the same time, there was an emphasis on social inclusion – 'They must be in no sense "professional libraries", or "tradesmen's libraries", or "working men's libraries", but TOWN LIBRARIES,' as Edward Edwards of the British Museum Library told the Select Committee.

The emphasis, then, was on self-improvement and on men, working men in particular, in towns. It was not until 1919 that a new Public Libraries Act allowed County Councils to become library authorities and make provision for people in rural areas.

Dissatisfaction with the first Public Libraries and Museums Act brought a further Act in 1855 which allowed towns governed under local Improvements Acts, and parishes, to become library authorities, and it allowed the authorities to provide the books and newspapers. At public meetings, there had to be a two-thirds majority in favour before the Act could be adopted, and if ten or more ratepayers demanded it, a poll of all ratepayers had to be held. It raised the amount that could be levied for library purposes to 1d. in the pound.

The take-up was slow, with only 35 authorities adopting the Act in the 1850s and 60s. Then came a gradual acceleration: by the end of the 1870s, the number had risen to 83, by the end of the 1880s to 153, by 1899 to 314, and by 1909 to no fewer than 522 authorities.

READING'S FIRST PUBLIC LIBRARY

The initial impetus to have the Public Libraries Act adopted in Reading came from an unexpected direction. In 1869, The Hon. Auberon Herbert offered money to several Berkshire towns towards the setting up of libraries. He was the brother of Lord Carnarvon, who lived at Highclere Castle, near Newbury. Reading was offered £250, on condition that a further £250 was raised locally. A 'committee of gentlemen' was formed to raise the £250, and a public meeting was held in the Town Hall on 14 February 1870. (The Town Hall would have been what is now the Victoria Hall, originally built in the 1780s.) Quite why this attempt failed is not clear – more than enough promises of donations were received to raise the £250, but it would have required a great deal more than £500 to build a library, even in 1870.

One who had been at the public meeting, and was dissatisfied with the outcome, was William Isaac Palmer. He was the youngest of the three Palmer brothers (George, Samuel, and William Isaac) who built up the Huntley and Palmer enterprise to become the biggest biscuit bakers in the world. He decided to take matters into his own hands, and set up a free public library in West Street, at his own expense, to demonstrate the need for a public library in Reading. Once the argument had been won, and Reading Corporation adopted the Act, Palmer donated the stock of the West Street library to the new institution.

A meeting of ratepayers to decide on adopting the Act was held in the Town Hall in 1877. The decision to adopt was almost, but not quite, unanimous. The scheme was to have the library and museum in the same building, plus rooms for the Schools of Science and Art, which would attract a government grant. Another committee was formed to collect the necessary subscriptions, but once again, all was not plain sailing. Their efforts were not as successful as they had hoped, and they had to go back to the councillors, and ask for £10,000 out of public funds. A group of councillors who were opposed, called a further meeting of ratepayers. The meeting called for a ballot of all ratepayers, which took place on 13 February 1879. The result was 1,675 in favour of paying the £10,000, and 336 against.

Door handles, Battle Library

Appropriately, when the Public Library and Museum Committee was set up in 1882, William Isaac Palmer was the first Chairman, a post he held up to his death in 1893.

The new library was opened in stages – the news room on 16 October 1882, the reading room on 1 January 1883, and the lending library on 12 February 1883. The site was adjacent to the new Town Hall, now called The Concert Hall. The library was on the ground floor, with the museum above. There was a major extension opened in 1897, to the north of the site, fronting Valpy Street, with a new news room on the ground floor, and an art gallery above. These arrangements remained more or less the same until the present Central Library at the corner of King's Road and Abbey Square opened in 1985. The removal of the library made way for the museum and art gallery to extend into the space formerly occupied by the library.

BRANCH LIBRARIES

By the 1880s, the population of Reading was growing steadily, and terraces of houses were stretching out along and between the main roads. The Oxford Road is a case in point, as is the Newtown area on the other side of Reading. Over the river, and at the time in a different county, Caversham was becoming in effect another suburb of Reading.

For those living in the new suburbs, the distance from the Free Library in Blagrave Street was one problem: another was the great pressure on space when they got there. It had on average 2,000 visitors a day, and pressure was particularly intense in the evenings. The reading room was open until 10 pm, six days a week.

The two branch reading rooms were a temporary and short-lived attempt to solve the problem. The Public Library Committee took over a room at Oxford Road Board School in February 1888. It was to have its own entrance, and its own gas supply – for lighting, because its opening hours were from 6 to 10 pm, six days a week. The average attendance soon rose to 110 people a night.

This initial success caused the Public Library Committee to do something similar for the east of Reading. They took over a room at the Earley Board School – now known as New Town School. In this case, the attendance was disappointingly low. It was decided to close the East Branch reading room for part of 1889 – July, August and September. When it re-opened in the autumn, the average attendance was only 33 people per night. This was reckoned too few people to be worth the expenditure, and this reading room closed completely from January 1890.

The Oxford Road reading room continued, but not for much longer. The average quarterly cost to the council was:

Reading Gas Company (lighting)	£4 9s. 1d.
Farrer and Sons (newspapers)	£1 14s. 3d.
Frederick Golding	£0 8s. 4d.
(magazines and books)	
School Board (caretaker's wages)	£3 18s. 0d.
TOTAL	£10 9s. 8d.

This meant that the total annual expenditure was £41 18s. 8d. Even so, the future of the reading room was called into question at the Public Library Committee meeting of April 1892. Average attendance was 60 per night, more in winter and fewer in summer.

The following year, 1893, the Public Library Committee proposed closing the reading room from the beginning of May to the end of August. It looks as though the re-opening on 1 September did not happen, because in May 1894 a petition was received calling on the Committee to re-open the reading room. The signatures of 439 people living nearby had been obtained by a Voluntary Committee. The local residents said that the reading room had been a great boon to the neighbourhood, and that the £50 or less a year was money well spent. The response, which did not come until November, was that 'having regard to the present state of the Library Funds, the Committee do not see their way to re-opening the Reading Room.'

Over at Caversham, a reading room had been open since 1883, with a lending library. They operated until 1911, when, presumably, much of their purpose had been taken on by the new public library. They were funded by Caversham Parish Council, and were housed in the Parish Room in Gosbrook Street – now Gosbrook Road. The building still stands, next to the car-park of the Clifton Arms public house, and is now the Cancer Care charity shop.

Use of these facilities was not free: to use the reading room you had to pay an entrance fee of 6d. and a subscription of a shilling a quarter. It was open between 6 and 10pm, Monday to Friday, and between 2 and 10 on Saturdays. It was open to all above the age of 18, and was 'supplied with daily (morning and evening) local, illustrated, comic, and other papers, journals and periodicals … Various games – chess, draughts, dominoes, etc. Smoking is allowed.' By 1900, it had a bagatelle table.

The lending library had very limited opening hours: 'Books will be given out every alternate Wednesday in the Parish Room, at 12 o'clock.' This could not have been of much use to people out at work, unless they worked close by. The subscription was 1d. a month, and the library was advertised as being 'non-political,' 'unsectarian,' and 'open to all.'

There was still a great need felt for a local public library, especially since, from about 1902, the munificence of Andrew Carnegie had made this more feasible through the offer of grants towards library buildings. In that year, Dr J. B. Hurry approached the Reading Free Library and Museum Committee, and various prominent Caversham residents, to persuade them to take up the offer.

Voluntary Committees were set up, independent of the local authorities, in Caversham and west Reading, to collect the signatures of ratepayers and to campaign for public libraries on the rates.

Caversham seems to have been first off the mark, led by its chairman, William Bullivant Williams, and honorary secretary, J. St. L. Stallwood. By November of 1904, the Voluntary Committee had presented the Urban District Council with a 'memorial' containing the signatures of 550 electors, asking for the Public Libraries Act to be adopted. The U.D.C. felt that, since

Window, Caversham Library

not everyone would use the library and be willing to pay the extra penny in the pound on the rates, the scheme should not go ahead.

Undeterred, the Voluntary Committee set about collecting more signatures, and also promises of money towards funding the library. Mr Stallwood wrote to Andrew Carnegie in June 1905, and received a promise of £2,500 for the building. Caversham Urban District Council agreed to adopt the Public Libraries Act at their meeting in October 1905. In the end, there was an overspend of £75 on the building, a debt which was eliminated by a further grant from Mr Carnegie.

Reading between the lines of the u.d.c. minutes, it would seem that the Voluntary Committee was reluctant to let go the reins. They paid over the £244 9s. 8d. they had collected to the Council only when requested to do so in July 1906, and were keen to become

involved in running a voluntary subscription scheme for the library in 1907, until instructed not to do so by the Council. The Voluntary Committee was wound up in July of that year.

Over at Reading, the Central Library was still suffering from overcrowding. The Corporation had applied to Andrew Carnegie as early as 1903, and had received the promise of £8,000 for two branch libraries, one in the east and one in the west of the town. Carnegie's secretary then asked for facts and figures. The branch in the east was to be near Cemetery Junction – the site where the Arthur Hill Memorial Baths were later built, and the one in the west was to be on the site in Oxford Road which was subsequently purchased. The population to be served by the new libraries was 20,000 in the east, and 13,000 in the west, with both communities steadily increasing. The secretary replied that he could not see how a penny rate would raise enough to support a central

A roof-light behind a fan-light, Battle Library

library and two branches. The Corporation promised to promote their own Act of Parliament to enable the rate to be increased from 1d. to 1½d. in the pound.

The Parliamentary Bill was drafted and deposited, but the local ratepayers still had to approve it. A meeting was summoned in January 1904. Although the vote was in favour of the Bill as a whole, a poll of all ratepayers was demanded. They were asked to vote separately on each of the seven sections of the Bill. Section 6, dealing with finance, was lost, meaning that the whole Bill had to be withdrawn, and the Carnegie offer could not be taken up.

As was the case in Caversham, it was an enthusiastic Voluntary Committee which swayed Reading Borough Council in the end. It was set up at the beginning of 1905, with Mr E. P. Collier as Chairman, and Dr Hurry as treasurer. A letter was written to Andrew Carnegie, asking if, in view of the failure to secure an Act of Parliament to raise the library rate, he would be prepared to make a grant for one branch library only. An affirmative reply was received, and a letter was written to the Borough's Public Library Committee in February 1906, asking them to accept Mr Carnegie's offer. The Public Library Committee refused, and the matter went to the full Council.

The Borough Council over-ruled its committee, but imposed two conditions: (1) that the site and the building were to be provided at no cost to the Council; and (2) that the Voluntary Committee was to provide £200 a year for the first three years towards the running of the library.

There was further correspondence between the Borough Council, Mr Collier, and Andrew Carnegie's private secretary over whether the penny rate would be sufficient to maintain even two libraries. Eventually, Mr Collier received a letter to say that, since Mr Carnegie believed Mr Collier to be the official representative of the community in this matter, Mr Carnegie had instructed his bankers to release the money. One suspects that it was not always easy for the private secretary to know quite which committee he was dealing with!

The Voluntary Committee went ahead, and raised the £759 for the site, next to the Union Workhouse in Oxford Road. (After the Second World War, the Workhouse was to become Battle Hospital.) They raised more than the necessary £600 towards the maintenance, and so fulfilled both the stipulations. They even appointed the contractors and oversaw the building operations.

It is sobering to realise the amount of determination, effort, and hard-won cash from private individuals that it took to secure branch libraries which are now taken for granted. Now that we have Lottery funding, and public/private finance initiatives, we expect everything to be provided as of right, and perhaps under-value what we already have.

ANDREW CARNEGIE, AND OTHER BENEFACTORS

The name 'Carnegie' is synonymous in this country and the United States with the funding of works for the public good – especially colleges and public libraries. The Carnegie United Kingdom Trust also made grants towards the purchase of church organs.

Andrew Carnegie (1835–1919) was born in humble circumstances near Dunfermline, Fife, the son of a weaver. He was a self-made man, and his story is extraordinary. His family emigrated to the United States during the 'hungry forties,' but he prospered, and became the owner of the Carnegie Steel Company, and was reckoned to be the richest man in the world. In 1901, he sold the company to J. P. Morgan's U.S. Steel Company, and devoted the rest of his life to giving away much of his fortune, claiming that it was a disgrace for a man to die rich.

As a young man, he had developed a passion for reading, helped by a Col. James Anderson, who gave him and other young working men in Allegheny access to his personal library. This, of course, was to have repercussions across this country and the United States.

He gave grants for the building and equipping of public libraries, if the local authority would give the site, and would guarantee the running and maintenance of the library. As we have seen, he would also ask questions about catchment areas and population, and about the product of a penny rate.

In the early years, he made the decisions himself, and a private secretary dealt with the correspondence – it was James Bertram who dealt with public libraries in this country. Sometimes Mr Bertram worked from New York, and sometimes from Skibo Castle, the Carnegie country estate in Scotland. When necessary, telegrams went back and forth. Then in 1913, he established the Carnegie United Kingdom Trust to administer the funds. By the time of Carnegie's death, in 1919, there were over 300 public library buildings paid for by him in the British Isles. Where public libraries were concerned, he had single-handedly transformed the situation in this country.

As we have seen, Caversham Urban District Council received £2,575 to build the library, and

Andrew Carnegie

Reading Corporation no less than £4,000 to build its West End Branch, later to become Battle Library.

The two libraries in Reading which are the subject of this book were not the only libraries for which Andrew Carnegie paid – Reading Central Library was also the recipient of his generosity. The Central Library was so busy that it was judged to be too small for the needs of the town as early as 1912. In that year, the Corporation instructed the Town Clerk to write to Carnegie to ask for a grant towards the cost of building a new central library in Reading. It was not until 1985 that a replacement was opened! The trustees replied that they had received so many applications for funding, that consideration of this one would have to be deferred.

In 1915, desperate for funds in the middle of the First World War, the Reading Public Libraries Committee asked the Town Clerk to apply to the Carnegie Trustees to ask for a grant of £1,000 towards reducing the debt on the existing Central Library building. The Trustees, understandably, wrote to ask whether this request cancelled their previous one for a replacement building. The Council replied that their previous request still stood. The Trustees offered the £1,000 as requested, on condition that another £1,000 were raised locally, which would extinguish the debt on the existing building. In addition, there was to be no reduction of the penny rate, and all the money saved on loan repayment costs was to be spent on books. The councillors agreed to the terms. They had a bequest from George William Palmer, eldest son of George Palmer and Chairman of Huntley and Palmers, who had died in 1913, which could be used to provide the additional £1,000.

The problem of the Central Library building did not go away, of course. The Town Clerk was asked to write to the Carnegie Trustees in September 1918 and again in November 1920, about their willingness or otherwise to defray the cost of a new Central Library. The reply of the Trustees is not recorded in the Library Committee minutes. By now, the priorities of the Trust had changed.

Jamieson Boyd Hurry

Hurry (1857–1930). After qualifying, he went to sea as a ship's doctor, before settling in Reading in 1885, aged about 28. He founded the Reading Pathological Society, and was interested in the links between housing, poverty, and human health. Two of his books, *Vicious Circles in Disease*, and *Poverty and its Vicious Circles*, went through several editions, and were translated into several languages, including Chinese and Japanese.

Outside his medical career, he had an interest in economic plants – he kept a collection of plants and a small museum at his house in Southcote Road. He took an interest in education, was a member of the council of the University College, and had a gymnasium built for the College. But it is his interest in Reading Abbey for which he is chiefly remembered today. Obviously a man of some wealth, in 1909 he presented to the town the memorial cross to King Henry I which stands in the Forbury Gardens. He commissioned the series of ten large paintings showing scenes from the history of the abbey, and presented them to the town. His classic history of Reading Abbey was published in 1901.

In his promotion of branch libraries, in Caversham he contacted influential residents, and called a meeting in the vicarage, which led to the formation of a Voluntary Committee, with William Bullivant Williams as chairman and J. St. Laurence Stallwood, a solicitor, as honorary secretary. Over in West Reading, he himself served as treasurer to the Voluntary Committee, with E. P. Collier as chairman. Not only that, but he purchased the sites for the East and West Branches, in case the branch libraries were built, though in the end, the East Branch came rather later, and on a different site.

To return to the beginnings of branch libraries, the man who took the initiative and started trying to make citizens aware of what was on offer from Mr Carnegie was a local physician and surgeon, Dr Jamieson Boyd

William Bullivant Williams

William Bullivant Williams (1835–1917), despite his impressive name, was by all accounts rather an unassuming character. He was an Oxfordshire magistrate, a sidesman of St. Peter's Church in Caversham, and a benefactor to Caversham in several ways. He was also opposed to Caversham becoming part of Reading Borough.

Educated at Reading School, he spent all his working life at Huntley and Palmers biscuit factory. Eventually he became Commercial Manager, and was invited to join the board. At one stage, he was the only board member who did not bear the 'Palmer' surname. He continued working until his last illness, only eleven days before his death at the age of 82. For many years he lived at 2 St. Peter's Hill in Caversham – a large house just above the footpath leading to The Mount.

As we have seen, he was the active chairman of the Voluntary Committee which had campaigned for a public library in Caversham. Besides donating the site – which had previously been the playground of the Caversham House Academy, across Church Street, and which was valued at £500 – he gave a further £500 to the project, paid for 1,000 books, and paid for the clock and its maintenance.

After laying the foundation stone of the Library, he was presented with a colourful illuminated address, which is now in the illustrations collection at Reading Central Library.

Among his other gifts to Caversham, he presented the site for the recreation ground in Caversham Heights, and the site of St. Andrew's Church there. Subsequently he paid to eliminate the debt on the church building.

Though not well remembered in these days – nothing seems to have been named after him – his funeral in 1917 was attended by many influential people from Reading and Caversham; so much so that arrangements were made for the police to control the crowd.

THE TWO BUILDINGS

Both Battle and Caversham Libraries are colourful, distinctive, and, on the outside, very much of their time. When the Central Library was being planned, in the 1870s, Gothic was the favoured style for municipal buildings. By the beginning of the twentieth century, things had changed. Although they are very different in appearance, it has been claimed for both buildings that they are in the 'Renaissance' style.

Both buildings are 'listed' as being of special architectural or historic interest under the Town and Country Planning Acts, and both are cherished by their local communities – though, as we shall see, replacement buildings have been proposed for both of them in the past. The combination of brick and stone dressings, towers, porches, gables, sculpture, clocks, turrets and stained glass makes these buildings decorative and lively, in a way in which the later branch libraries were not.

Ornamental ventilation turrets are a feature of both buildings, reminding us that at the time, the ventilation of public buildings was a major preoccupation. The prevalence of infectious diseases was one concern: mercifully they have now been virtually eliminated from this country. Also there were worries that gas lighting consumed the oxygen in the air and gave off noxious vapours. Mr Greenhough, Reading's Borough Librarian, had read a paper on the ventilation of public libraries to the Library Association when they held their annual meeting in Reading Town Hall in 1890.

The architects of both buildings were decided upon by competition. At Caversham, the Urban District Council asked the Royal Institute of British Architects for advice in running such a competition. The judges were the Reading firm of architects, Charles Smith and Son. Seven entries were received, and the winner, announced in July 1906, was a local architect, Mr W. G. Lewton. All the entries were displayed at the Police Court House in Church Road, opposite the Griffin Inn. At the time this would have been the Urban District Council's only public building. Mr Lewton lived in Woodcote Road, and he had many commissions for large houses on

SKETCH OF THE SUCCESSFUL DESIGN.

Caversham Library as planned by the architect

The exterior of Caversham Library today

The clock, Caversham Library

style. The significance of the word 'free' is probably that, unlike Battle Library, Caversham is not symmetrical, and that it uses elements from a number of different architectural styles. The stone canopy over the entrance is borrowed from the Queen Anne style, and the pillars supporting it are borrowed from classical architecture. The entrance doors, with their round windows, are reminiscent of the Arts and Crafts movement, as is the tapering clock tower above, with the corner turret surmounted by a green copper ball and a weather-vane in the form of a swan. A second green copper ball sits on top of a ventilation turret. On the official list of 'listed' buildings, it is described as 'sub-Voysey.' Charles Voysey (1857–1941) was a leading Arts and Crafts architect, noted for his slightly quirky designs, and for the fact that he liked to design everything down to the smallest detail – hinges, key-holes, window stays, door panels, wallpapers, etc. – so that all was in keeping. Something of this kind of detail remains at Caversham in the windows and doors. It would be interesting to see pictures of the original wood-panelled interior, but none seem to have survived.

The winged figure of Old Father Time, carrying his scythe, is often commented on. Though it is described as 'an Atlas figure' on the official listing, correspondence between the clerk of the Library Committee and William Bullivant Williams in February 1907 says that the Urban District Council 'will be pleased to pay the cost of carving the figure of Time.' The name of the sculptor does not seem to have been recorded anywhere, but the initials 'B. L.' are still discernible at the foot of the figure and to the right, in a good light.

Caversham Heights. The Reading Synagogue, in Goldsmid Road, is another of his public buildings. Built in 1900, like Caversham Library, it has a green copper ball on the top.

In the souvenir brochure of the opening ceremony, the library was described as being in 'Free Renaissance'

The swan weather-vane, Caversham Library

Mr Williams paid for the clock, and for its maintenance during his lifetime. The contractors were the well-known Reading firm, Bracher and Sydenham. As originally installed, the clock had a chiming mechanism, and was illuminated at night. A recent (2007) visit to the tower revealed no trace of the clockwork mechanism or the chimes, but a triangular funnel with a chimney to disperse the heat and fumes from three gas-lights was still there. The clock is now driven by electricity.

The original iron railings and gate which surrounded the library were sent away for salvage in the Second World War, and were replaced in 1946 by metal posts, and a chain-link fence with a privet hedge behind. The Borough Council thought better of its controversial attempt to open up the frontage in 2001, and after consultation with English Heritage, put back replicas of the brick gate-piers with stone balls on the top – even more piers than were originally there! The iron railings were also replaced, but this time with knobs on top, rather than spikes.

The strip of land surrounding the library has occasionally caused controversy. The almond tree to the right of the entrance has had to be replaced several times because it did not thrive. The planting of the very large tree on the Hemdean Road side of the building seems to have gone unrecorded. Botanically, it is *Sophora japonica*, an unusual species. In some summers it flowers profusely, and fills the air with scent. On the other hand, falling flowers and leaves regularly block the library's gutters, and make the pavement slippery in wet weather.

The West End Branch Library is more restrained in its architecture, and is symmetrical. The official listing describes the architectural style as 'Wrennaissance.' The design was again decided by competition, but in this instance, three firms of architects were invited to compete – W. R. Howell, W. G. Lewton, and F. W. Albury. The assessor was Mr W. Ravenscroft. The winner was the Reading architect, F. W. Albury, who had offices in Friar Street. Many of his buildings still stand in the town centre, notably the shops on the corner of Duke Street and King Street (Davina's news-agents, Douglas Jacobs the jeweller, and the Prospect estate agency), and those on the corner of Cross Street and Friar Street (Bradford and Bingley). He was also responsible for The Berkshire Club in Blagrave Street (later The Forum public house and now the Oakford Social Club) and The Corn Stores in Forbury Road.

The cupola on the top, part of the ventilation system, has a dome of lead, with a weather vane above.

Again like Caversham, the feature that draws forth most comments is the sculpture – the three heads on the gable above the entrance. Left to right, they are reckoned to represent Newton (though sometimes said to be Milton), Shakespeare, and Darwin.

THE WEST END PUBLIC LIBRARY.

The West End Library (later known as Battle Library) as planned by the architect

The exterior of Battle Library today

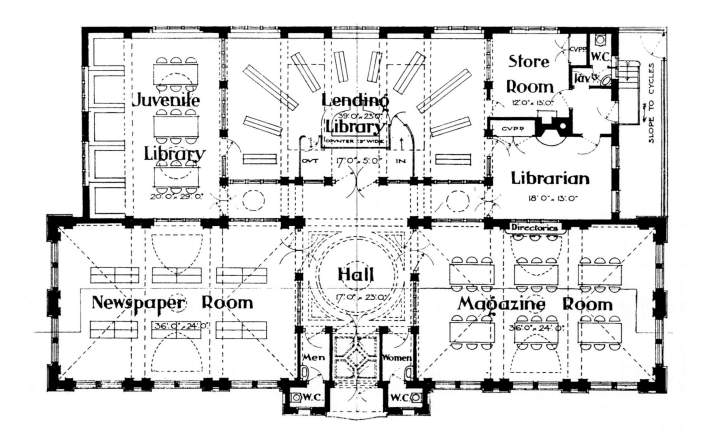

Plan of West End (later Battle) Library, 1907

Ground Plan.

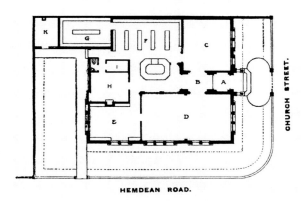

HEMDEAN ROAD.

CHURCH STREET.

REFERENCES.	ACCOMMODATION.

A. Vestibule
B. Hall
C. Magazine Room 22ft. × 19ft.6in.
D. News Room 37ft. × 20ft.

E. Reference Room 21ft. × 16ft.
F. Lending Library 32ft. × 21ft.
G. Book Store 21ft. × 12ft. 6in.
H. Librarian's Room 16ft. × 13ft.
I. Book Cupboard
K. Heating Chamber

28 readers
24 readers at tables;
20 at newspaper stands
10 readers & 1700 vols.
8000 volumes
5400 volumes

Plan of Caversham Library, 1907

This library has retained more of its period charm internally than Caversham. The entrance hall is lit by a sky-light of colourful stained glass, depicting the arms of Reading Abbey, Reading Borough, and the University College, Reading (later the University of Reading). The rooms to the left and right of the entrance have attractive barrel-vaulted ceilings.

Though there is no 'garden' at Battle Library, the paved area in front was improved, with ornamental lamps and seating, when the rest of this stretch of Oxford Road was given a face-lift about the year 2000. Stone paving was introduced, with quotations from Judah Ha-Levi and Sir Isaac Newton incised into it by Pip Hall. The unusual lamp-standards along the road were nicknamed the 'ball-cock' lamps when they first appeared.

From a glance at the floor-plans of the two buildings, both published in souvenir brochures of the opening, it is obvious that everything in the West End Branch was one size bigger than at Caversham, and that the West End Branch made provision for children, whereas Caversham didn't. The building at Caversham had cost £2,500, but that along the Oxford Road, £4,000. The plans also show that much more emphasis was placed on reading newspapers and magazines in the library, rather than borrowing books to take home. Another sign of the times was the fact that Caversham had one table in its magazine room reserved for the exclusive use of ladies.

FOUNDATION STONES AND OPENING CEREMONIES

The laying of the foundation stone at Caversham took place on Saturday 23 March 1907, in fine spring weather. William Bullivant Williams, the donor of the site, performed the ceremony. The mortar was spread with a presentation silver trowel, and the stone was tapped several times with a presentation mallet. In a cavity, there was placed a bottle, containing copies of the four local papers, and a parchment recording the munificence of Mr Carnegie and Mr Williams. Mr Frank Knighton proposed a vote of thanks to Mr Williams.

Dr Hurry, in his speech, said that 'he believed access to good books would help to check crime, add to the happiness and welfare of the people, make the workman a better workman, the artisan a better artisan, the teacher a better teacher, the scholar a better scholar.' A free public library, it had been said, was a 'palace of delight, in which those who would, could find refuge from many of the storms and worries of life.'

In his reply, Mr Williams said that 'They at Caversham would take great care that all books of a perni-cious character were kept out of the Library, but there must be a certain scope allowed for different tastes. He hoped the books would be of an edifying character, and would help those who read them forward in the march of life.' The ceremony ended with the singing of the National Anthem.

There must have been some differences of opinion among the people of Caversham. The Reading Standard, after printing a conventional account of the proceedings, added this postscript, in doggerel verse, headed 'On Laying a Foundation Stone.'

> The sun was shining brightly
> The banners streamed around
> When a little band of citizens
> Stood on crimson covered ground
> To lay a grand 'Foundation Stone'
> It was their fixed intent,
> And seriously and solemnly
> With heavy steps they went.

For this very doubtful blessing, for
Which the ratepayers will groan,
With a Herculean effort they
Upraised this wondrous stone,
And laid it safely down to rest
In a nicely plastered little nest,
And then they swelled to twice the size
(Unless the sun was in my eyes).

And then one made a little speech,
Which no-one near could hear,
And then they sang a little song
'Mid trembling doubt and fear,
And then they said ''Twas over, and
Outside we all must pass,'
We'd such a lot of policemen, and
We'd such a lot of gas.

The West Reading Branch Library was not so fortunate with the weather on Wednesday 16 October. The ceremony was carried out by the Mayor, Edward Jackson, and J. B. Hurry. Again, a silver trowel was used to spread the mortar, and the objects placed in the cavity included coins minted in 1907, as well as the local newspapers. Although the stone-laying took place under an awning, the inclement weather drove everyone into the Elm Park Hall Methodist Church next door for the speeches. The speech of Dr Hurry was much the same as the one he had made at Caversham in March.

The construction at Caversham must have raced ahead. At the time of the stone-laying, it was thought that the library would be completed in July. As things

The opening of West End Library

turned out, the official opening was not until Wednesday 11 December. For some reason, it was to take place at four in the afternoon, when it must have been dark. The recently formed Caversham Fire Brigade was on parade for the occasion. Viscount Valentia opened the front doors with a silver key, and the ticket-holders went inside for the speeches and presentations. An illuminated address was then presented to Viscount Valentia, who was the Chairman of Oxfordshire County Council. William Bullivant Williams presented a large framed portrait of Andrew Carnegie to the Library, and J. St. L. Stallwood presented a companion portrait of W. B. Williams. Mr Stallwood also presented an illuminated address to Mr Williams.

A souvenir programme was produced for the occasion, with an 'artistic' purple cover, designed and printed by Poynder and Son. A black and white photograph of the building was stuck on the cover.

The same firm produced the souvenir of the opening of the West Branch, this time a green cover, with dark green printing. The design featured a globe, a bust of Shakespeare, an ink-well and two quill pens, and a scroll.

The opening ceremony was on 3 June 1908, and was performed by the Rt. Hon. G. W. Palmer, with 'a handsome key.' The building was inspected, and people then went next door to Elm Park Hall for the speeches, presentations, and the tea which had been laid on by the Mayoress, Mrs W. M. Colebrook.

Dr Hurry, representing the Voluntary Committee, handed the deeds of the building to the Mayor, asking him to accept them on behalf of the town.

In his speech, Mr Palmer said that 'It was unnecessary in these days to speak of the advantages of public libraries, but he desired to remind the younger people that those advantages had not always been recognised, and that years ago it was only after patient, persistent striving that Reading people had been persuaded to adopt the Public Libraries Act.' It was his uncle, William Isaac Palmer, who had done much of the striving. He also mentioned the limitations of the penny rate, which 'did not give them sufficient money to enable them to carry on the work as they would like to.'

Ventilation panel in the ceiling, Battle Library

EARLY YEARS, 1907–1914

From the beginning, it was obvious that Caversham didn't have enough ratepayers and rateable value to run the library, and things were not much better in Reading, where the Committee was frustrated by the limitations of the penny rate. Many other councils across the land were finding themselves in the same position.

In Caversham, the penny rate brought in £145 a year. The salaries of the two members of staff took almost half of this – the librarian at £40 a year, and the porter at £28 6s. a year.

Even before the library opened, in July 1907 the u.d.c.'s Public Library Committee sent round a circular, appealing for 'voluntary subscriptions.' By January 1908, these had raised £35 14s., with a further £1 1s. promised.

Stringent measures were called for. The Committee decided that the lighting at Caversham was 'much too extravagant,' and reduced it. (When Reading Borough took the building over, they decided that the lighting was inadequate, and increased it.) The old newspapers were sold off by Frank Cooksey, the auctioneer in Reading Market Place, who obtained £1 2s. 6d. a year for them. When they received the rating assessment for the library, the Committee appealed, and had the rateable value reduced from £60 to £20 a year.

It may surprise some present-day residents that until 1911, Reading stopped at the River Thames, and everything on the other side was in Oxfordshire. Caversham was the place at the other end of the bridge, with its own Urban District Council. The arguments why Caversham should become a part of Reading were apparent in 1887, when Reading expanded to take in the built-up part of Tilehurst. By 1910, they were overwhelming, but even so, the u.d.c. was sticking to its policy of non-cooperation with Reading.

A household survey showed that half the households in Caversham made their money in Reading. Already, gas, water and electricity were supplied from Reading, and the Caversham sewage works in Amersham Road was barely able to cope with the increase in population. The new electric tramcars stopped on the Reading side of Caversham Bridge, because the Caversham u.d.c.

refused to finance the widening of the carriageways. And we have already seen the problems of a small local authority running a public library.

It is perhaps understandable that the Caversham councillors should wish to defend their 'village,' even though they must have known that incorporation was inevitable, and that, as J. St. L. Stallwood admitted, Caversham couldn't really afford to win its case for remaining separate.

At the time of the hand-over on 14 November 1911, the two branch libraries were costing £290 a year to run between them. In 1912 and again in 1913, the Reading Public Library Committee requested the Town Clerk to add a clause to the Parliamentary Bills which the corporation was promoting at the time, to allow the library rate to be increased by up to ½d. in the pound. This would have been politically unpopular, and the full Council was unwilling. The penny limit was finally removed across the country by the Public Libraries Act of 1919.

From reading the committee minutes, it looks as though libraries in Reading weren't even getting the product of the penny rate. In 1913, the Public Libraries Committee demanded that the whole amount raised should be spent on libraries. The full Council did not agree: £50 was to be used towards maintaining the Art Gallery.

If we could go back and visit these branch libraries at the time of the amalgamation, we would probably be surprised at the lack of popular reading. The selection of books, newspapers and magazines was in the hands of the Books Sub-Committee of the Public Libraries Committee. The main committee met monthly, and the sub-committee on alternate months, after the meeting of the main committee. They seem to have relied heavily on donations – the committee minutes have a list of donations appended every month. William Bullivant Williams had given 1,000 volumes to Caversham Library in the beginning, and the sub-committee had bought as many volumes as it could second-hand to save money. The result would have been a 'worthy' collection with many classic texts, but no bright covers, and not much to attract readers of popular novels, who may well have resorted to subscription libraries. Eight or nine of these are listed in directories of Reading, including Farrer's West Reading Library at 341 Oxford Road. Later, branches of W. H. Smith's, and Boot's the Cash Chemists had lending libraries of popular novels into the 1950s, and some local newsagents ran a similar service: the Argosy Library was one example. By the 1950s, public libraries were becoming more conscious of the piper calling the tune, and of their duty to serve the whole of the community, including 'low-brow' readers.

At least in 1911, we would have been able to browse amongst the books in both Caversham and the West Branch Libraries. In the Central Library, we would still have had to look on a board – the 'Cotgreave Indicator' – to see what was available, and ask for books at a window. A member of staff would then have gone off into the stack to find them. Whether or not the Caversham Committee heed the requests of the Caversham clergy that the racing information should be blacked out from the newspapers is not recorded.

The children's library of the West Branch (later Battle) Library, around 1910.

Also, in 1911 we might well have had difficulty in finding our way around. The Dewey Decimal Classification had not yet been adopted, and each branch had a different alphabetical classification. At Caversham, the classification began: A – art and science; B – biography; C – essays; D – poetry and drama; E – natural history; F – fiction … and so on. At the West End Branch, we can see from the photograph of the lending library that class N was drama, class O was history, and class P geography. The Dewey Decimal Classification was not adopted at all Reading's libraries until 1937.

We might also be surprised to find different rooms in the libraries open at different times. The reading rooms at Caversham opened from 8 am to 10 pm, Mondays to Saturdays. The newspaper and magazine room opened from 1 to 4 and 6 to 9, so you couldn't read the morning paper till lunch-time. The lending and reference libraries opened 3 to 4 and 6 to 9. At the West Branch, hours were slightly less generous, but still lavish by today's standards: 9 am to 9 pm for the reading rooms, and 3 to 4 and 6 to 9 for the lending library.

The lending library of the West Branch (later Battle) Library, about 1910.

Another difference from the present day would be the absence of a children's library at Caversham. The West End Branch, as we have seen, had a 'juvenile library' from the start, but over the water, the Urban District Council had decreed that children under 14 were not to be admitted to the library at all. This now seems very misguided, when for so many years public libraries have put so much effort into developing literacy and 'the reading habit' through special schemes, and making children's libraries particularly colourful and attractive. Children's books were first provided at Caversham in 1912, though there was not to be a children's library until 1948.

Other measures, too, were necessary to bring Caversham into the fold. Record-keeping had not been up to scratch, and much of the book-stock was in need of repair and re-binding – not surprising if much of it was obtained second-hand in the first place. It seems that, in order to save on the cost of gas, the reference reading room was often locked at night, but Reading decreed that it should be kept open and lit. Library tickets could now be used at any of the three public libraries in the Borough, and copies of the printed catalogue of the Central Library were to be made available at the branches.

Communications, too, were to be improved: initially, the Urban District Council had refused the National Telephone Company's offer to install an instrument in their library. Now, Caversham was to have a 'telephone call cabinet, on the penny in the slot system' for public and staff use – the same as at the West End. And a bicycle was purchased, to enable staff to travel from one branch to another.

In later years, it used to be said that, for sending 'unofficial' messages between the two branches, members of staff would at an agreed time stand on top of their buildings, from where they could see one another, and signal by semaphore! Today, there are too many tall buildings in the way.

Opening hours were standardised – reading rooms 8 am to 9 pm, and lending libraries from 2 to 4 and 6 to 9. So you still couldn't borrow a book in the morning.

In a typical year before the First World War, the West End Branch lent 21,000 books, and Caversham lent 20,000. This compares with around 42,000 books at Battle Library, and 146,000 at Caversham today.

Neither branch employed a professional librarian: they could not have afforded to. Only the Chief Librarian at Reading was qualified at the time. At Caversham, besides being the librarian, Edward Boyer Hobbs was a stationer and toy dealer at 31 Prospect Street – the shop is now occupied by Caversham Herbs. His shop is listed in street directories until 1921, the year before his death. The porter, Mr H. T. Watling of 5 West View Terrace, wore a uniform provided by Frank King, tailor, of Church Street. The words 'Caversham Public Library' appeared on the hat-band. The porter did not get on with Mr Hobbs, 'because Watling did not adopt himself to the particulars required,' and was sacked in 1909. One wonders if either of them ever took a holiday, and is vaguely staggered by the unsociable hours they must have worked. After the hand-over, Mr Hobbs was to be there from 1 to 4 and 6 to 9, six days a week, and Mr Watling from 7 to 11 am and 7 to 9 pm. Before that, they must both have been there till 10 at night!

There are three fine photographs of the two libraries in these years. Unfortunately, no pictures of the interior of Caversham Library seem to exist, but the two of the West End Branch are particularly good. The gas-lit 'juvenile library' is occupied largely by boys in Norfolk jackets, and the titles of the magazines are legible on the original – *Chatterbox*, *Child's Companion*, *Band of Hope Chronicle*, *Band of Mercy*, *Child's Own Magazine*, *Chums*, etc. The lending library has a barrier across the entrance: presumably it was operated by the librarian behind the counter. Some of the suspended signs can be read, to give us an idea of how the library was

arranged, and the umbrella stand in the foreground, with space for twenty umbrellas, is particularly impressive. The picture taken on coronation day – 22 June 1911 – is one of the most evocative photographs of Caversham Library. Mr Hobbs, the librarian, had himself paid for the loan of the stuffed lion, which had to be brought from London – presumably a symbol of British supremacy. It stands in the porch, with the letters 'G & M' above, standing for King George V and Queen Mary.

From the committee minutes comes an interesting side-light on the history of Caversham: St. Anne's Well on Priest Hill was restored in 1908, and at the meeting of 30 April of that year it was agreed to accept a display case of the relics dug up in the process. Later, they were to receive some further archaeological relics – Roman pottery discovered when All Hallows Road was constructed. Hopefully the relics are now safe in Reading Museum.

These were the golden, pre-war years, when it must have seemed as though material progress would never cease, and the lot of working people would continue to improve.

Far left: Caversham Libary on Coronation Day, 22 June 1911

35

THE WAR YEARS, 1914–1945

The first mention of war in the Public Libraries Committee minutes comes in the September of 1914, when it was reported that one of the library porters had enlisted. War had been declared the previous month.

It soon became apparent that the war would not, as some had imagined, be over by Christmas, and great numbers of wounded men were being returned to England, in need of care. In February 1915, the War Office was demanding over 1,000 'military beds' in Reading, in addition to what the Royal Berkshire Hospital could offer. These were to be provided partly by taking over school buildings, but mainly by taking over most of the Union Workhouse in Oxford Road. Arrangements were made for the transfer of the existing inmates to neighbouring unions, and the conversion of the Reading Workhouse to a war hospital.

By the middle of 1916, it was apparent that even more beds were needed: the campaign on the Western Front was bringing in a flood of casualties.

In October of that year, the officer in charge of the Reading War Hospital requested that the West Branch Library, which was adjacent to the hospital, should be handed over to the War Department. The Council agreed, and the books and furniture were put into store, and the building was handed over on 27 November.

It took a long time after the end of the war for things to revert to normal. In 1918 came the influenza epidemic, and many of the Reading victims died in the War Hospital. A marquee had to be erected in the grounds, to act as a temporary mortuary. Rumour has it that the West Branch Library was also used as a mortuary, though no documentary proof seems to have survived.

In March 1920, the closure of the War Hospital was announced, and it seemed likely that the library would be handed back, but now the Ministry of Pensions stepped in, and asked if they could take over the tenancy, 'for, inter alia, the continuation of special out-patient orthopaedic treatment for pensioners who required it.' The corporation conceded, and offered a tenancy, to be reviewed quarterly, at a rent of £250 a year. The Ministry said they wanted a five-year lease to justify the expenditure on adapting and equipping the building. Among other things, electricity was to be laid on. The Corporation declined, and the quarterly arrangement went ahead.

By the middle of 1922, pressure was mounting for the library to be re-opened. In reply to a letter from local residents demanding to have their library back, the Public Libraries Committee wrote that it had been let to the Ministry of Pensions, 'for the purpose of special out-patient orthopaedic treatment for war pensioners, and the Committee do not see their way, owing to existing financial conditions, to recommend the Council re-open the library at present.'

In November, the Mayor received a petition from 204 local residents. The Public Libraries Committee decided to defer consideration of the matter until their meeting of February 1923, but the situation changed in December, when the Director of Lands and Accommodation, H.M. Office of Works, wrote to say that he intended to deliver back most of the building on or before 25 March 1923. He wanted to retain only a part of the building, and this was agreed, at a rent of £50 a year.

Following repair and redecoration, the newspaper and reading rooms of the West Branch Library re-opened on 22 October 1923. West Reading had been without a library for almost seven years. The Ministry of Pensions had vacated the building completely by March 1924.

Over at Caversham, the library seems to have remained open throughout the war. All libraries had reduced opening hours, closing at 8 pm instead of 9, and all had to obey the Defence of the Realm Regulations, and black out their windows at night. There was a police complaint about Caversham's black-out in 1916, which had to be addressed.

During the First World War, the Borough Librarian reported that the libraries were busier than ever – the two that were open, at any rate. Just before the war, the West Branch had issued round 21,000 books a year, and Caversham around 20,000. Book loans at Caversham were now 1,000 a year higher than in peace time, and the daily papers were in great demand, as were books about the war. In fact the statistics show that the rise in book issues at Caversham was comparatively modest – around 5%.

The practice whereby the books, magazines and newspapers were selected by a sub-committee seems to have come to an end about the same time as the war came to an end, without any formal resolution having been made.

The end of alphabetical classification systems, and the adoption of the Dewey Decimal Classification came about in both branches in 1937.

The inter-war years saw great improvements in children's libraries. Changes were made at the West Branch, and a new 'juvenile department' with a dedicated children's librarian was created. The former children's library was to be used by the schools' library service. Of the new children's librarian it was stipulated that 'in addition to the usual educational qualifications, it will be necessary that she should be in sympathy with all that concerns children's reading and recreation, attractive to children and able to interest them, yet an excellent disciplinarian … '.

Today, it seems odd that it should be assumed that the children's librarian would be female. The 'disciplinarian' who was selected, Miss Pattenden, seems to have been an excellent choice.

The new children's library was opened by the Mayoress on 29 October 1935. 'In this airy, spacious and well-lighted room, book-stacks of a height suitable for children have been installed … An excellent stock of the best books for young people has been provided … An experienced children's librarian is in charge of the department. In 1936, it was reported that library talks for 11–14 year-olds, and story hours for 8–11 year-olds took place regularly, and the new room was 'thoroughly well organized and increasingly well appreciated by the children using it.' There had been film shows, and an exhibition of model aeroplanes. It is interesting to note that the local paper felt the need to explain that 'it is the practice in all fully developed children's libraries to arrange such a series.'

At Caversham, there was a children's reading room for magazines, but the books for borrowing were still shelved in the adult library. The children's activities took place there as well, but it wasn't until after the next war that Caversham had a new children's library and a specialist librarian. At this time, children could join the library from the age of 8, and a new scheme was introduced so that parents could have special tickets and take out books for younger children.

Throughout the Borough's libraries, reading rooms were open from 9 to 9, six days a week, and lending libraries from 10 to 8, except on Wednesdays, when they closed at 1, Reading's traditional early closing day for shops.

Another matter exercising the Public Libraries Committee during the inter-war years was out-of-borough borrowers. The libraries could be used by any visitor for reading and reference, but the borrowing of books was available only to electors, ratepayers and residents. If you lived in Berkshire, the County Council had a lending library in Abbey Street which you could use, but if you lived in Oxfordshire, there was no provision. The boundary between Caversham and Mapledurham was less than a mile from Caversham Library, and for many people living in Sonning Common, Kidmore End, etc., Caversham and Reading would have been the places to go shopping, or to work.

In 1921, a scheme was introduced so that anyone who was not otherwise eligible could use the public libraries in Reading, on payment of a deposit of £1, and an annual subscription of 2s. 6d. The deposit was waived if you obtained the signature of a Reading elector or ratepayer as guarantor. If you failed to return a book, either the deposit was forfeit, or the guarantor would be called upon to pay. The annual subscription was raised to 5s. in 1923. Then in 1937, an arrangement was reached with Oxfordshire County Council, whereby the County Council paid 3s. towards the subscription, leaving the borrower to pay the remaining 2s.

It was not until the 1960s that Berkshire County Council gave up their lending library in Reading, and came to an arrangement with the Borough Council.

With both branch library buildings around twenty years old, some repairs were necessary, and some minor improvements were made in the 1920s and 30s. The heating systems and the flooring at both libraries needed attention. At Caversham, the flooring was of 'doloment' – a compound of magnesite, sawdust and silica, and it had to be patched, and eventually replaced. At the West Branch, the problems were caused by minor subsidence of the building itself, on its sloping site. The telephone 'call cabinets' were removed in 1924, and ordinary telephones installed for library staff. The electric light came to Caversham in 1931 – the West Branch had received it by courtesy of the Ministry of Pensions.

In 1932, the Committee gave permission for Caversham Library to be used as a polling station, if no other accommodation could be found, and for another display case to be installed at Caversham, for the exhibition of Roman and other remains.

The build-up to the Second World War was more apparent to all than the build-up to the First. The Borough Librarian was seeking advice about air-raid precautions and his powers to close libraries in an emergency towards the end of 1938. By this time, he had three additional branch libraries to worry about: East Branch, later called Palmer Park, in St. Bartholomew's Road; South Branch, later called Whitley Library, in Northumberland Avenue; and Tilehurst Branch, in Armour Hill – not the present library in School Road.

At the beginning of the war, the opening hours of all the branch libraries were curtailed, so that closing time for all departments was 7 pm, whereas it had formerly been 8 pm for lending libraries, and 9 pm for reading rooms. Even to the present day, we have never returned to the generous pre-war opening hours.

The West and Caversham branches were busier than ever, on account of the evacuation scheme. Wilson School had an influx of children from London, which meant that the Reading children had use of the school for one half of the day, and the London children for the other half. The junior department of the West Reading Branch was open from 10 to 12.30, and from 1.30 to 6, for the children who were not in school. 'At this time, the room has been taxed to its utmost capacity,' the Borough Librarian reported. There must also have been an influx of evacuees in Caversham, because some of the rooms there were taken over by London school teachers. The Borough Librarian calculated that the evacuation scheme had added 2,517 new borrowers to the register, most of them schoolchildren.

The two libraries played their part in other smaller ways to the war effort. An Air Raid Precautions (A.R.P.) Wardens' post was built behind the West Branch, and before it was built, the wardens could use the boiler room and the cycle room at the library. The porter's room was used as a rest-room for special constables on night duty.

A room at Caversham Library became the headquarters of the 'A' Group of the Civil Defence Wardens' Service, and the library was used as a registration centre in connection with the Civil Defence Duties (Compulsory Enrolment) Order 1941. Men who had not so far been called up, or who had registered as conscientious objectors, were now liable to be called upon to perform full-time work of a civilian nature, and under civilian control, and they would be deemed to be serving the Crown, and paid a wage. Also, in 1942, the branch libraries were used for the distribution of ration books, while the children's reading room at Caversham was

Round window in the front door, Caversham Library

taken over by the Ministry of Food, 'for the duration,' and used to store sugar. At this time, the opening hours of branch libraries were curtailed even further, closing at 6.30 on Mondays, Tuesdays, Thursdays and Fridays, 7.30 on Saturdays, and 1.00 on Wednesdays.

An invitation to submit reminiscences of the two libraries brought in this amusing story of war-time Caversham – an incident which could so easily have had tragic consequences. A boy was cycling down Hemdean Road to the library, and was approaching the corner of Chester Street, when he heard an aircraft roaring overhead. Incendiary bombs began to fall, one of them on the pavement on the opposite side of the road. It was about eighteen inches long and two inches in diameter, and began to burn fiercely. Others had fallen on nearby

rooftops. 'I don't remember being scared, but rather amazed', he recalls. For a few minutes he watched people gathering sandbags, expecting a bombing raid. Then he cycled on to Caversham Library to change his Biggles books, totally naively. There he was surprised to be confronted by an irate librarian who said: 'Go away, boy, we've got bombs on the roof, for goodness sake. Come back tomorrow.' So he cycled back home in a state of some excitement. When he explained to his aunt what had happened, she just said: 'Nonsense, boy. There were no air-raid sirens. Stop telling stories.' 'That's how it was in the war', the correspondent recalls, 'People just got on with their lives, and for children who had hardly known any other lifestyle, the bizarre was almost commonplace.'

RECENT TIMES, 1945–2007

Before going any further, it may be as well here to explain the changes in the management and in the nomenclature of the public libraries in Reading. The Local Government Act of 1972, coming into effect on 1 April 1974, gave the control of public libraries in shire counties to the County Councils. Boroughs that wished to keep a measure of control over their libraries could come to an agency agreement with the County Councils, and in Berkshire, Reading was the only borough to take this option. The agency agreement lasted for only a few years.

It was during Berkshire's stewardship, in the late 1970s, that the then Divisional Librarian, Ian Lewis, decided to change the names of some of the Reading branch libraries. The West Branch became Battle Library, the East Branch became Palmer Park Library, and the South Branch became Whitley Library. The new names are much more descriptive of where the libraries are, and of the communities they serve.

The government made a further round of changes to the local government system in the 1990s. It had long been recognised locally that the boundaries of greater Reading meant that much of its population lived in adjacent Rural Districts: Bradfield (parts of Tilehurst) or Wokingham (Woodley and Earley). Now, it was thought, would be the time to remove the anomaly. There was a public consultation, which offered only two options, so there was some consternation when the government announced that it was to implement a third option – an option that was not tried anywhere else in the country. The County Council was to be abolished, and the area to be run by six comparatively small unitary authorities, of which Reading was one. Reading was to keep the old boundaries of the County Borough, so that a large part of its built-up area was still outside its boundaries. The new unitary authority came into existence on 1 April 1998, with a central library and six branch libraries, as it had before 1974.

To pick up the threads of our story, after the end of the war, a Public Libraries Post-War Reorganization and Development Sub-Committee swung into action, and one of its main aims was the creation of a children's

The children's library at Caversham, Christmas 1949

library at Caversham, and the appointment of another children's librarian. Once the Ministry of Food had released its hold on the old children's reading room, this could become the new news room, and the old news room could become the children's library.

Another concern was the poor state of the children's books across the Borough, after six years of low spending, restricted availability, and books being produced to a war-time economy standard. A spending programme was implemented, and by June 1948 the number of children's

Children's author Grace James visits Caversham Library, 1949. The children look strangely apprehensive.

books being borrowed across the town had doubled, compared with a year before. The new children's library at Caversham was opened by the Mayor on 24 June.

Hand-in-hand with the improvements to the stock of children's books, there was a new programme of events for children. At the West Branch, they were on Tuesdays, and at Caversham on Fridays. As well as talks and story hours, there were now quizzes, play-readings and puppet-shows. Of the book quiz held at the West Branch, which attracted 60 children, the Borough Librarian wrote in his report: 'I had a riotous evening.' There were calls for it to repeated. Over 100 children were present at the visit of Grace James, the children's author, to Caversham Library in 1949.

We are never likely to see again those heady days, before television, play stations and the internet, when hordes of children turned up – but activities for children are still popular, and at Battle Library, the 'Sing along' sessions have proved very successful. At both libraries, for toddlers there are 'Rhymetimes,' for 3–5 year-olds, 'Story times,' and for older children, 'Chatterbooks' reading groups.

In the 1970s and 1980s, we had Children's Book Weeks, with events held at different branches, including visits from authors and theatre companies. A Carnival Disco, part of the 1983 Caribbean Week, saw youngsters doing the conga round Battle Library. More recently, libraries have played their part in the Reading Children's Festivals, and in the Bookstart programme, which encourages parents to read to their young children.

Perhaps, at this stage, it is worth remembering that although the buildings of both Battle and Caversham libraries are almost icons for their communities, serious consideration has been given to replacing both of them with newer buildings on different sites at different times. This was done with the best of intentions – providing modern buildings which were cheaper to maintain, and, in the case of the overcrowded Caversham Library, bigger buildings.

In 1971, the Borough Council was considering what to do with Grovelands Primary School, in view of falling pupil numbers. One proposal was to combine it with a new public library, and to close down and sell the old library building.

Over the water, in 1972, a new library, combined with a health centre and an adult education centre was pro-posed for Caversham. The plans came to nothing, and it is still fair to say that Caversham Library is bursting at the seams.

In 1991, at one of its fairly regular panic meetings over funds, the County Council considered closing 18 of its smaller libraries permanently – Battle Library included. It is hard to know how seriously this was considered, and whether this was just one threat being used to ward off another threat, and whether the councillors were just trying to gauge how hostile the electors would be to the loss of branch libraries.

In 1992, under the headline, 'Library Shocker,' the Reading Chronicle reported that one of the options for the redevelopment of the Battle Hospital site was to replace the old building with a new one. 'The Library Service finds the building expensive to run,' one county councillor said. By this time, the building had been listed by the Department of the Environment, so it was fairly safe.

Over the last sixty years, the library buildings have been used for various purposes, and sometimes for purposes which have nothing much to do with libraries. In 1956, for instance, the Registrar of Births and Deaths hired part of Caversham Library, for a payment of £26 a year. Unfortunately, the committee minutes don't specify how much space was taken up.

The West Branch was a considerably bigger building than Caversham, and the intention to use part of it as a bindery was first put forward in 1949. Initially, the bindery had been in the basement of the Central Library, and moved to the West Branch in 1952. It served Reading Borough for around 50 years, closing in 2000.

It dealt with around 6,000 volumes a year, and could do the work rather cheaper and faster than external contractors – but in-house services in local authorities were no longer fashionable in the 1990s.

For a time, in the 1970s and early 1980s, the county drama collection was held at Battle Library. This was a collection of play sets, which could be borrowed by amateur dramatic societies. It had previously been at the County Library Headquarters – Abbey Mill House, in Abbey Square. In 1985, when the new Central Library was opened, it was re-housed in the County Music and Drama Library there.

In the present century, Battle Library has played host to various activities to promote health: ante- and post-natal clinics, a baby clinic and a breast-feeding clinic are regularly held. It also works with schools, and the Berkshire Community Drug Agency, and has sessions for job-seekers. A carol service for the community has become a regular event, and recently, there have been coffee mornings, with visiting speakers.

The arrangements with neighbouring local authorities over out-of-borough residents continued after the war. In the 1960s, Berkshire County Council was considering a new large office building in Reading, between the River Kennet and King's Road, which would involve the demolition of their Headquarters Branch Library. Berkshire agreed to pay Reading Borough £3,500 a year, to give Berkshire borrowers the free use of Reading libraries. This did not, however, apply to people living in boroughs with their own library services, such as Newbury and Maidenhead. When someone joined the library, the member of staff had to ascertain precisely where the person lived. In the case of Oxfordshire, it was even more complicated. Oxfordshire County Council agreed to pay £1 a year for each borrower registered with Reading, and they paid quarterly. Rather than just dividing the number of Oxfordshire borrowers by four, the staff at Caversham Library had to punch out holes in the pink cards for Oxfordshire readers, which showed the quarter in which the particular borrowers had joined the library. Then, once a quarter, they did an exercise involving long knitting needles, which hooked out the cards that had been punched in that quarter. This administrative nightmare was much simplified when Berkshire County Council took over the running of all the public libraries in the county in 1974. In 2007, when public libraries are keen to register as many people as they can, the old arrangements look laughable.

From a glance through the collection of newspaper cuttings about the public libraries, maintained at the Central Library, it would seem that during the post-war years, the libraries have lurched from one financial crisis to another. There have been almost constant threats of cuts to opening hours and services. Sometimes they have been implemented, and sometimes, after public protest, they have not. Occasionally, lost opening hours have been restored, and even improved on. One cannot help but feel that if the funding for public libraries were just slightly more generous, and could be relied on to stay about the same in real terms, year on year, vast amounts of energy and ingenuity could have been expended on much more positive activities than producing reports and arguing at meetings to protect the service, implementing reductions in service, occasionally reversing them, and causing general heart-ache among the staff.

One or two instances will suffice to illustrate the point. In 1961, all branch libraries were to close for 1½ hours at lunch times, to save £400 a year in staffing costs. At most, if not all of them, lunch times must have been the busiest times. Lunch-time opening has been restored at Caversham Library, though not yet at Battle.

The Divisional Librarian's report for 1979–80 makes particularly dismal reading. After talking about reduced budgets, and reduced expenditure on books, he says: 'Most outreach and promotional activities for children and adults have ceased.' In 1986 came the proposal to close all branch libraries on Saturday afternoons. Of course, the reason for this is that under a long-standing agreement, the staff are paid at time-and-a-half on Saturdays. Petitions were received from users of various branches – 471 people signed up at Battle Library. Some councillors argued that at some of the libraries, a quarter of all their transactions were made on Saturday afternoons, and their argument prevailed.

All has not been doom and gloom, and in the latter part of Berkshire County Council's stewardship of the library service, great improvements were made in the book stocks everywhere. But the threats do not go away, and in local government, the public library service is often seen as the Cinderella, still awaiting the Fairy Godmother.

It seems a pity, in this quick skip through the history of the century, to feel obliged to mention the decline in standards of public behaviour. This, of course, mirrors what was happening in the country as a whole. Before the 1970s, problems with break-ins, vandalism, drug abuse and theft in libraries were almost unknown. There may have been unruly youngsters, but nothing that could not be dealt with by the staff. At branch libraries in particular, there have been small gangs of youngsters who take delight in intimidating whoever they can – other youngsters, customers, and staff. Libraries have to take what measures they can to prevent disruption and protect people and property.

Now, perhaps more than ever, public libraries are keen to engage with the community, to raise their profile, and to prove their worth. Both libraries, for instance, have played host to councillors' 'surgeries' on Saturday mornings, where people can meet their elected representatives.

Caversham Library has a presence at the Caversham Festival, held on the Westfield Road recreation ground in September, while Battle Library has contributed to the West Reading Festival. Among the many and varied events, there has been an exhibition on transport in Reading, an exhibition about Mary Seacole, and a dramatised presentation on the history of the Library, to celebrate its 90th anniversary. More recently, the library has been one of the initiators of the Oxford Road Community Festival.

For many years, there has been a 'One World Week' exhibition in Caversham Library. Each exhibition has a different theme: in 1986 it was 'Living on the Edge,' which looked at the plight of people living on the edge of society, locally, and in Reading's twin town of San Francisco Libre in Nicaragua. Pupils from Highdown School wrote essays on the subject.

The two branch libraries serve very different communities. In general, Caversham is one of the wealthiest parts of the borough, and the area of west Reading served by Battle Library is one of the less wealthy parts. But this is only a generalisation, and Caversham has its own areas of social deprivation. The library at Caversham is particularly well positioned, in the middle of the shopping centre: Battle Library is on the main road in this part of town, and is about to have a large supermarket built next to it. The Tesco effect could be to bring in many more customers for the library.

The stock in both libraries – DVDs and periodicals as well as books – varies according to the people who live in the neighbourhood. As different groups of people have come to live and work in Reading, so the stock has changed. Battle Library has a long established and well used collection of books in Urdu, along with the Daily Jang newspaper. Recently, a shelf of books in Bengali has been added, and its use is being monitored. After the Second World War, Caversham Library had a collection of books in Polish, for the families of the men who served in the Allied forces, and who were living in camps in the Chilterns just north of Caversham at the end of the war. Over time, the number of loans decreased, as the older generation declined or moved away, and only a small collection in the Central Library remained. Then in 2004, after Poland joined the EU, the shelves of books on Polish were quickly emptied, and spending had to be increased to meet demand. It is hoped this year to return books in Polish to branch libraries – this time to Battle Library, since many of the new generation of Poles live off the Oxford Road.

Caversham now has a small but steady group of readers for books in Urdu. Books in Chinese were popular here a few years ago, when there was an influx of students, but demand has tailed off, though books in Hindi and Bengali are well read.

From the 1980s onwards, the march of technical innovation has become increasingly apparent in libraries. To consider firstly the way in which book loans are recorded, for years and years the Browne system sufficed. This was the system by which the library card was a little cardboard envelope, bearing the reader's name and address, and each book contained a card bearing its details. When someone borrowed a book, the card from the book was slipped inside the library card and stamped with a return date. The envelope, complete with book-card, was then filed in a tray in date order. When the book came back, the library card was handed back and the book-card slipped back inside a pocket at the back of the book.

In the 1970s, the system in branch libraries was simplified by 'token charging.' Each borrower was given a number of tokens which could be exchanged for books, and there were separate tokens for fiction and non-fiction. The tokens looked like a half-sized plastic credit card. If you lost a book, you could pay a standard charge for a replacement token. The big disadvantage was that if another person wanted to reserve a book, you had no idea of who had it out, so all reservations had to be dealt with at the Central Library. Computerised issue systems arrived in the branch libraries in the late 1980s.

The way in which you could look at the library catalogue, too, has been transformed. Originally, there was a printed catalogue of the stock at the Central Library. Until the 1970s, there were also typed catalogue cards in drawers in a cabinet, but only for the one particular library. Then after the take-over by Berkshire in 1974, there was access to the complete county catalogue, on microfiche. The miniaturised catalogue was printed onto panels of transparent plastic, which needed an illuminated magnifier in order to read them.

Then, in the late 1980s, the branches were also connected to BVS – the Berkshire Viewdata Service. This was based on the technology that ran Prestel – the tele-text system used by television companies to provide viewers with an additional information service via their TV sets. It was a forerunner, of course, of the internet, and would appear terribly slow and limited if we had it today. Berkshire County Libraries ran it, on behalf of the County Council, and it was a fore-runner in its day. It provided access to the library catalogue for the whole county (though not on-line access), lists of local societies, a 'what's on' calendar, lists of local companies, lists of job vacancies from job centres, and information from various government departments, including the Central Office of Information, and the Department of Health and Social Security. It also ran a children's magazine, with jokes, stories, and a question-and-answer service. Before Christmas, you could use it to send a message to Santa Claus – a source of great amusement to mischievous adults as well as children!

About ten years later, in the late 1990s, the internet had arrived, quickly taking over much of what was on BvS. The Library website filled the gap, and continued to give access to what needed to be provided locally – such as the catalogue, and local societies. Eventually, it provided on-line access to the catalogue and circulation system, which meant that borrowers could see what they had on loan, and could renew the loan on books they hadn't finished with, so long as no-one else wanted them. Later improvements have meant that you can now order items to be kept for you, and look at pictures of places around Berkshire in years gone by.

At first, internet access was expensive to provide. When Battle Library got its first terminal in 1997, there was one terminal only, and it cost £5 an hour to use it; print-outs were 25p a page. The government's 'People's Network' initiative has meant that many more terminals are available, free of charge, and printing is 15p a page.

Alongside this transformation, new ways of storing audio-visual material arrived, and formats became available which were suitable for lending from libraries. The analogue formats were just too vulnerable: digital formats are rather more robust. The audio cassette has come and gone, replaced by the compact disc, or CD, just as the video cassette has given way to the digital versatile disc, or DVD, all within the space of a few years. The growing availability of down-loadable material from the internet, the ease of access to it and paying for it electronically, probably means the eventual end of pre-recorded programmes on disc, and of a whole industry, and of the shops that sold the discs.

THE FUTURE

As this book goes to press (October 2007) it has been announced that the Library's bid to the Big Lottery Fund to carry out alterations to Battle Library, as part of the Community Libraries Programme, has been successful. The impact of this additional funding, plus the impact of the arrival of a supermarket and car parking nearby will transform the service.

The intention of the bid is to make the library much better used, and more relevant to the whole of the community living in the area. What were formally staff areas will be refurbished and brought into community use, so that a large variety of activities can take place. While retaining its architectural distinction the building's negative impact on the environment will be reduced – it will be more energy efficient and cause less pollution. A new community garden is to be created.

As mentioned in the previous chapter, Battle Library already has a wide range of activities for different sections of the West Reading community within its walls. Additional activities proposed include children's art and craft sessions, a homework club, a maths and science club, and an IT-based study support scheme for primary age children, English speaking classes, and parenting classes. All this will be achieved in two years: perhaps this, or something like it, will be the way forward for all public libraries.

But what of the future of the traditional book-based service? One of the great unknowns for people who enjoy reading is the future of the book as a physical object. If an electronic device with a flat screen comes on the market, which doesn't have to be connected to a power supply by a cable, and which is pocket-sized, light, and can contain the text of one or several books, and is fairly cheap, will we still prefer paper and cardboard? Even when this device is produced, it seems unlikely that there will be anything as satisfying as flipping back and forth in books to find the bit you want.

It may well be that soon most people in this country will have their own internet access, so there will be no need for public terminals in libraries. They will download music and images from the internet, and won't want to borrow pre-recorded material.

So far, statistics show that the printed book is holding its own … .

SOURCES

Alexander, Ian. *Borough Government and Politics: Reading 1835–1985*. 1985
Reading Central Library reference: R/F

Caversham Urban District Council. Letter books, 1905–1911
Berkshire Record Office reference: UD/CV/CDI/1–2

Caversham Urban District Council. Public Library Committee. Minutes, 1905–1911
Berkshire Record Office reference: UD/CV/CBI/1

Caversham Urban District Council. Souvenir of Opening of the Public Library at Caversham … 1908
Reading Central Library reference: RH/GD

The ephemera collection, in the Local Studies collection at Reading Central Library

Greenhough, William H. *The County Borough of Reading. The Public Libraries. A Retrospect of Thirty Years, 1882–1912*. 1913
Reading Central Library reference: R/GD

Hart, Richard J. *History of Reading Public Library, 1877–1908*. Unpublished typescript, 1967
Reading Central Library reference: R/GD

The illustrations collection in the Local Studies Collection, Reading Central Library
Much of it can be viewed on the library website: www.readinglibraries.org.uk

Jones, Sylvia E. W. *80 Years +: a Brief History of Caversham Library*. Unpublished typescript, 1988
Reading Central Library reference: RH/GD

Munford, W. A. *Penny Rate: Aspects of British Public Library History, 1850–1950*. 1951

Newspaper cuttings files, and microfilmed copies of the Reading local newspapers, the *Chronicle*, *Mercury* and *Standard*, in the Local Studies Collection of Reading Central Library

Railton, Margaret, and Barr, Marshall. *Battle Workhouse and Hospital, 1867–2005*. 2005
Reading Central Library reference: R/JXA

Reading Borough Council. Free Library and Museums Committee. Minutes, 1908–1909
Reading Central Library reference: R/GD

Reading Borough Council. Free Libraries Committee. Minutes, 1909–1910
Reading Central Library reference: R/GD

Reading Borough Council. Public Libraries Committee. Minutes, 1910–1957
Reading Central Library reference: R/GD

Reading Borough Council. Cultural and Entertainments Committee. Minutes, 1958–1961
Reading Central Library reference: R/GD

Reading Borough Council. Public Libraries, Museum and Cultural Committee. Minutes, 1961–1966
Reading Central Library reference: R/GD

Reading Borough Council. Public Libraries and Museum Committee. Minutes, 1966–1972
Reading Central Library reference: R/GD

Reading Borough Council. Amenities Committee. Minutes, 1972–1974
Reading Central Library reference: R/GD

ACKNOWLEDGEMENTS

I should like to thank Reading Libraries, who invited me to write this book; Marjorie at Battle Library and Vij and Matt at Caversham who have given me access to their buildings and brought me up-to-date on one or two points; present-day colleagues at the Central Library, who have given information and advice in their own areas of expertise; and Sylvia Jones and Richard Hart, two former members of staff, who did a lot of the spadework on the history of public libraries in Reading. The collections in the Berkshire Record Office have been invaluable in sorting out the early history.

Thanks are due also to the publishers, Two Rivers Press, and especially to the designer, Nadja Guggi.